piano / vocal / guitar

ISBN 978-1-4234-3928-8

HAL•LEONARD®
CORPORATION
7777 W. BLUEMOUND RD. P.O. BOX 13819 MILWAUKEE, WI 53213

Visit Hal Leonard Online at
www.halleonard.com

FALLING SLOWLY

Words and Music by GLEN HANSARD
and MARKETA IRGLOVA

Slowly ♩ = 69

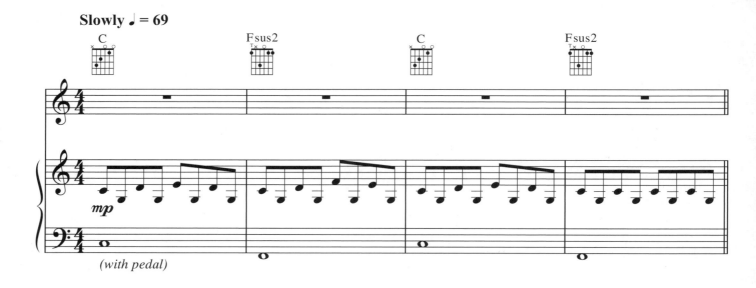

Verse 1:

1. I don't know you, but I want you all the more for that.

Words fall through me and al-ways fool me and I can't re-act.

IF YOU WANT ME

Words and Music by
MARKETA IRGLOVA

BROKEN HEARTED HOOVER FIXER SUCKER GUY

Words and Music by
GLEN HANSARD

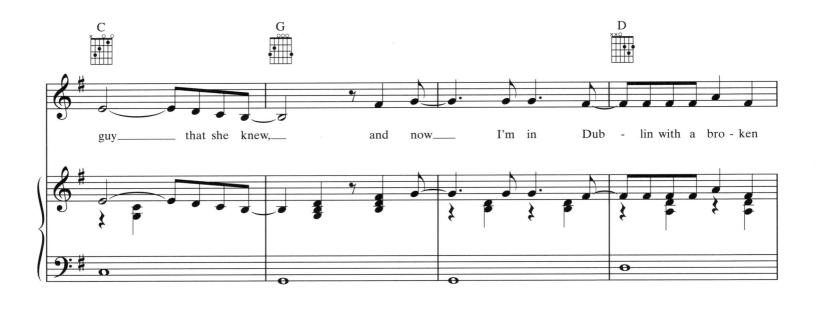

guy_____ that she knew,____ and now____ I'm in Dub – lin with a bro – ken

Chorus:

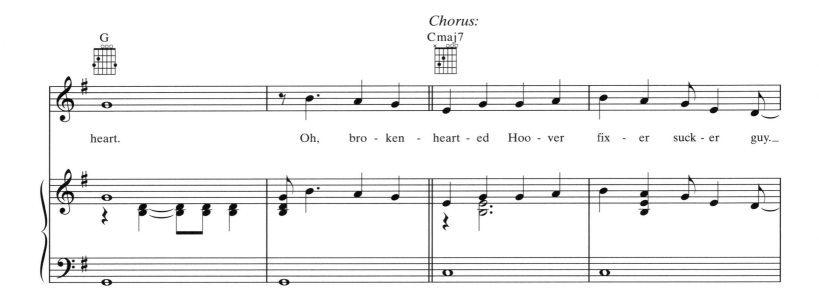

heart. Oh, bro – ken – heart – ed Hoo – ver fix – er suck – er guy.___

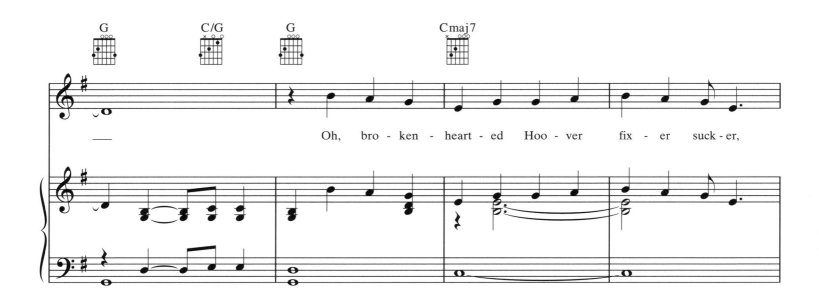

Oh, bro – ken – heart – ed Hoo – ver fix – er suck – er,

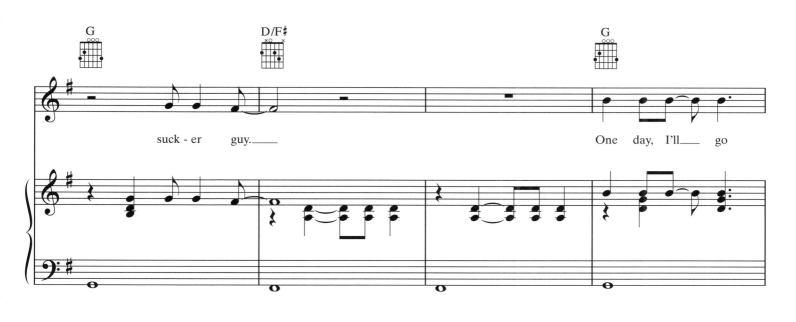

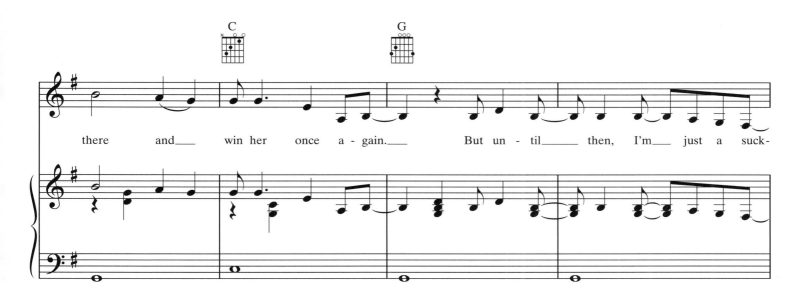

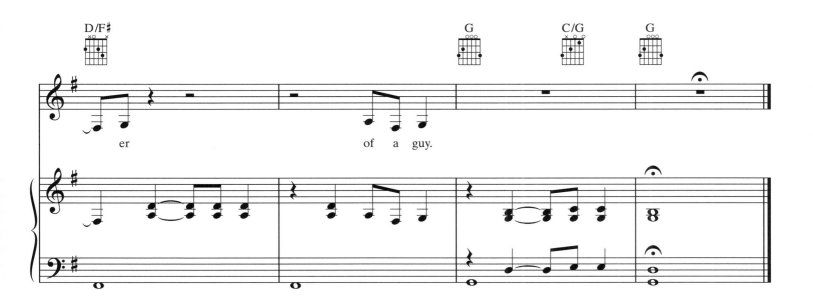

WHEN YOUR MIND'S MADE UP

Words and Music by
GLEN HANSARD

LIES

Words and Music by GLEN HANSARD
and MARKETA IRGLOVA

GOLD

Words and Music by
FERGUS O'FARRELL

Moderately fast, in 1

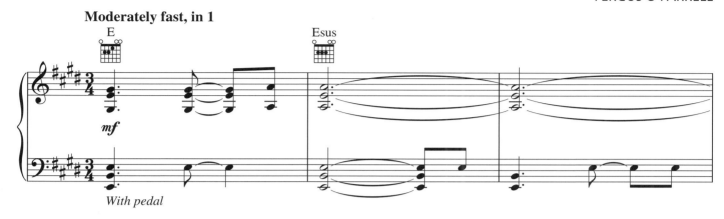

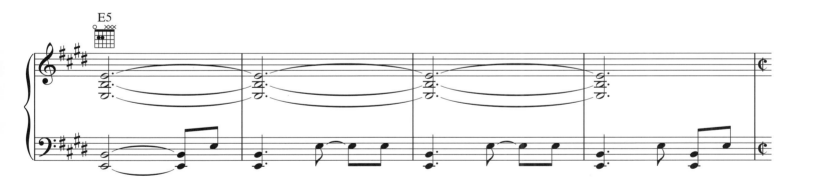

1st time only: **Hey!**

Esus

Hey! __

1

E5

THE HILL

Words and Music by
MARKETA IRGLOVA

Look-ing   at   you leav - ing,   I'm look-ing for   a   sign.

FALLEN FROM THE SKY

Words and Music by
GLEN HANSARD

Chorus:

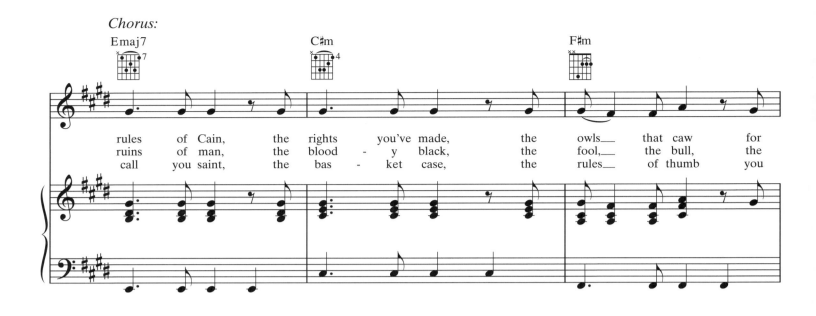

rules of Cain, the rights you've made, the owls___ that caw for
ruins of man, the blood - y black, the fool,___ the bull, for the
call you saint, the bas - ket case, the rules___ of thumb you

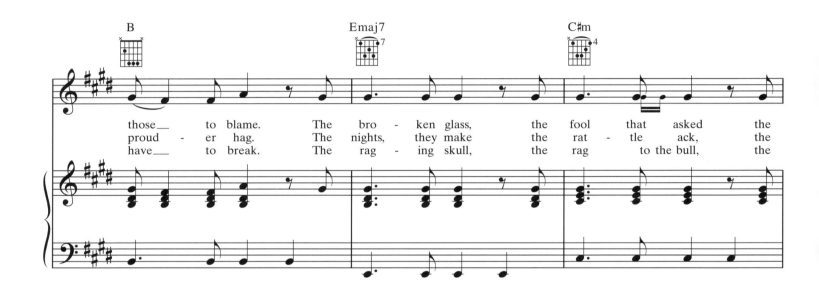

those___ to blame. The bro - ken glass, the fool that asked the
proud - er hag. The nights, they make the rat - tle ack, the
have___ to break. The rag - ing skull, the rag to the bull, the

To Coda

mov - ing ar - row to stop. 3. You must - 've fall - en from the out - ed man. The
wolves___ that fol - low the
nails___ that drag___ in

LEAVE

Words and Music by
GLEN HANSARD

* Standard E frame 2nd verse.

TRYING TO PULL MYSELF AWAY

Words and Music by
GLEN HANSARD

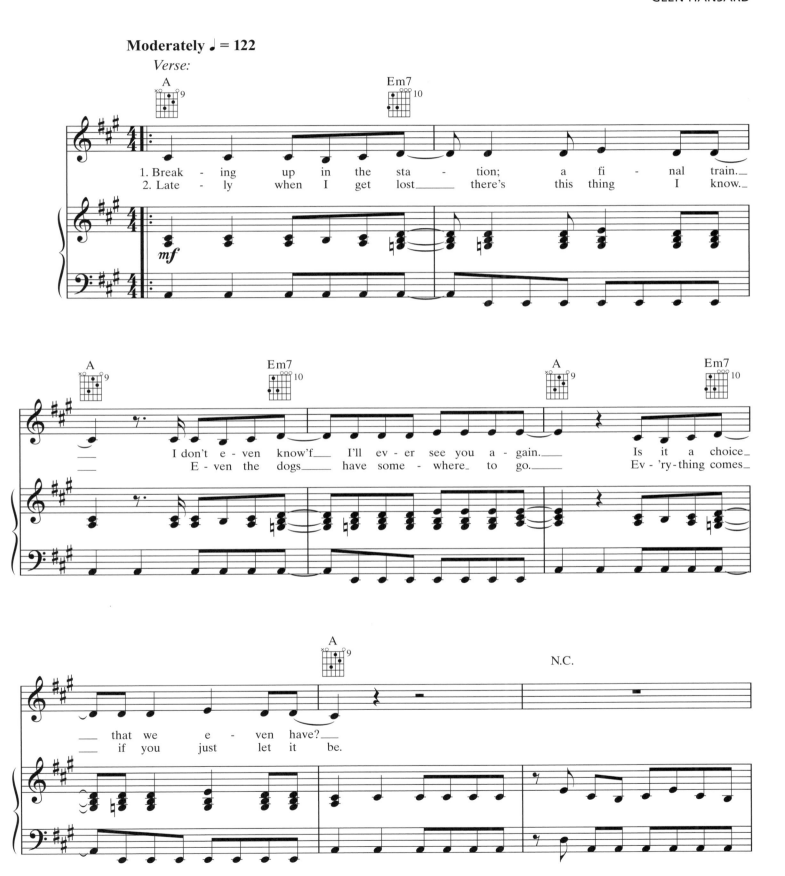

Chorus:

ALL THE WAY DOWN

Words and Music by
GLEN HANSARD

ONCE

Words and Music by
GLEN HANSARD

Gm F C
the part that's burned.
Chorus:
Am7 D7(4) F C
Once, once, knew how to talk to you.
Am7 D7(4) F C
Once, once, but not an-y-more.
cresc.
Dm7 Am7 Em7
Hear the si-rens call me home.
mf

SAY IT TO ME NOW

Words and Music by PAUL BRENNAN,
GLEN HANSARD, DAVID ODLUM,
GRAHAM DOWNEY and NOREEN O'DONNELL

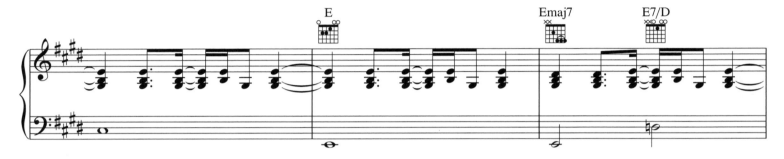

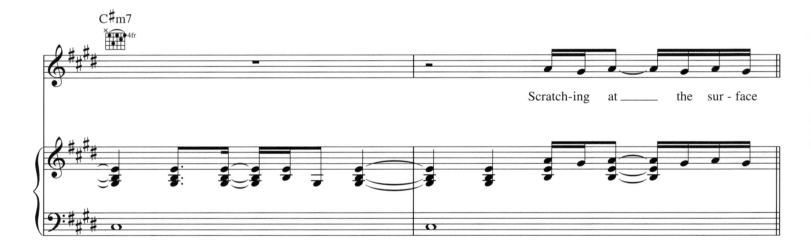

Scratch-ing at _____ the sur-face

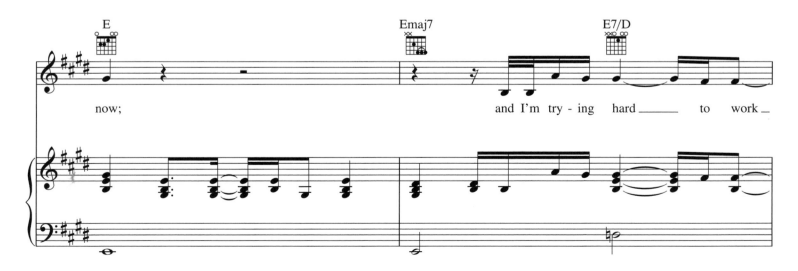

now; and I'm try-ing hard _____ to work _